22 B

PRAISE FOR *HOLDING UP THE MOON*

Marsha's haiku hit me right between the eyes and blow my heart open. She has made the form her own in a powerful, surprising, and exquisite way.

~Joyce Rasmussen, Writer in the Haiku Room

Marsha Pincus awakens us to the power of brevity in storytelling—how much can be said in so few words, and how beautifully. Her memoir is as much about the power and mystery of language and imagery as it's the story of how one woman moves through life, with a heart that's both broken and brave enough to love still and again. Keep oxygen nearby, because every page will steal your breath away!

~Jennifer Leigh Selig, co-author of *Deep Creativity: Seven Ways to Spark Your Creative Spirit*

Marsha takes to the Haiku as naturally as bees pollinate flowers. But, there is something distinctive she is doing with her haikus. The twists and turns of relationship, language and love, dreams and time, and yes, nature too of course, are all refreshed, renewed and put squarely in front of you as parts of a woman's individuation journey. The complexity of these haikus asks first that you read them all the way through and then that you sit with them a while and watch how they open and blossom in your own garden.

~Angelo Spoto, Jungian Psychotherapist

Marsha writes with such beauty that I am overwhelmed with a sense of gluttony. She invites us to dream along with her as she writes of family images buried in our flesh, the scars of lovers inscribed on our hearts, and the ever-persistent emotional desires rolling in our gut. Her haiku remind me of a *Canto Hondo*, a Flamenco-style song that emanates from the very depth of a person's soul.

~Shirley Munoz, Ed.D,
Teachers College, Columbia
University, Educator

In these beautifully constructed emotional haikus, Marsha Pincus tells us, in ways we won't forget, what it feels like to be a woman in her sixties, full of powers of observation, honesty, and love.

~Esther Cohen, Poet

What a delight to spend time with Marsha's words and the images they evoke! So wise and witty in the most elegant way. Nearly all of the haiku vibrated, resonated in my body, like only special poetry does.

~Dianne Jenett, Ph.D., Transformative educator, co-author of *Organic Inquiry: If Research Were Sacred*

I feel such gratitude for Marsha's haikus. They are an invitation: a poetic exploration of the evolution of Marsha's soul, and an invitation to the images that connect us all.

~Carla A. Kleefeld, Ph.D.
Psychotherapist, Educator

Marsha's haiku are so lovely, and speak of the shadows in a woman's soul.

~James T. Baker, Singer/Songwriter

Any memoir that Marsha writes will have a style that grips the reader. Whether expressing herself in haiku or prose, Marsha's command of the language offers a witty, artistic, and deep read.

~Peggy Cook, M.Ed., Teacher, artist, and author of *Released: Walking from Blame and Shame into Wholeness*

Marsha Pincus is on fire! Her haiku are powerful. So few words pack a huge reaction. So excited to have them together in this collection.

~Nadine Rosen Levin, Educator

When I met Marsha Pincus in 1987 I was inspired by her teaching, but also the way she told stories of her teaching and wove through them the stories of so many wonderful young people in her classroom in Philadelphia. Once again she has led the way for me (and others), as she continues to tell her story, in a new phase of her life, in ways that help all of us find our own voices.

~Dina Portnoy, Ph.D., Activist

HOLDING UP THE MOON

A Memoir in Haiku

Marsha Rosenzweig Pincus

Copyright © 2022
Marsha Rosenzweig Pincus
All rights reserved
978-1-950186433

Starry background photo by Paul
Volkmer on Unsplash
Two Ravens logo designed by
Michael Amundsen

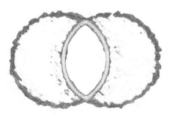

MANDORLA BOOKS
WWW.MANDORLABOOKS.COM

DEDICATION

To M. - *all ways, always*

INVITATION

In 2014, I was part of a Facebook community of writers who pledged to write and share a haiku a day for a year. The invitation came from Nicole Galland, a writer whom I had met the previous summer at a retreat for women writers in New Mexico, organized by A Room of Her Own Foundation (AROHO). Nicole had given herself this challenge and invited others to join her in "The Haiku Room," primarily for accountability.

Turns out The Haiku Room was far more magical than that.

The Haiku Room grew to over 200 members, primarily women, though there were also some men among us. The rules were simple. We agreed to post one haiku a day, offering only encouragement and positive feedback. The haiku would conform to the traditional seventeen syllables, but our topics could move outside of the natural world elements required of traditional Japanese poems. The writers in the Haiku Room created a community where we examined emotions like grief, loss, and joy. We shared our inner lives, long-lost memories, and epiphanies. The haiku challenge came at a very unstable time in my life. I had become an empty nester, a retired educator, and a restless wife. The persona of *wife-mother-teacher*, which had held my world together for the previous 30 years, began to shatter around me. I was in the midst of my second Saturn Return, and nothing in my life was making sense. I began to feel despair about my future. I had never written a haiku in my life, nor did I have a daily writing practice, but something intuitively nudged me to accept this challenge and bring this sort of structure into this chaotic time.

On January 1st, 2014, I wrote my first haiku and tentatively posted it to The Haiku Room and my personal Facebook page:

we grow into our
ancestor's hardened faces
with each faded dream

I was overwhelmed by the generosity of the responses I received and inspired by the range, creativity, and depth of the haiku posted by others. So I wrote another. Then another. During that year, I learned how to show up for my own muse and how to be present for the creativity of others. This presence opened the door of our shared sacred space for poetic discourse, creative playfulness, and soulful exploration. My haiku began to give words and images to the pieces of my broken identity. Eventually, they paved the way for the descent into my psyche. There, I confronted memories from my childhood, ghosts of my ancestors, and powerful archetypal energy. The haiku helped alchemize my fears into seventeen syllables of gold.

For one whole year in this interactive community, we engaged each other's psyches, danced with each other's muses, and followed the threads of each other's inner journeys.

I posted my 365th haiku of 2014 on December 31st:

who could imagine
so much could be carried by
aching syllables

I had met the challenge I'd taken on at the beginning of the year. I was done. The process, however, was not done with me. On January 1, 2015, I posted a new haiku. And so it continued. Writing and sharing my haiku had not only become my writing practice-it became essential in my journey toward healing and wholeness. For the next seven years, I would continue to post my haiku to my Facebook and Instagram communities.

I am grateful to the members of those communities who encouraged me to put this book together.

Holding Up the Moon is a collection of 92 haiku culled from over 2500 I wrote during those years. The challenge, of course, was not only how to select them, but how to arrange them. I began the process by printing each haiku onto slips of paper. I selected the ones that had the most meaning and energy. Then I laid those out on the floor and waited for them to find their way to each other. They told me where to move them and I followed their lead, eliminating, arranging, and rearranging the haiku until they ordered themselves into the story in this book.

I know there are many other stories that those 2500 haiku could tell. I see the haiku as pieces of colorful shreds of paper inside a kaleidoscope–this book is just a snapshot of one combination, 92 pieces of confetti poised in the mirrors–turning the barrel would reveal another story.

And doesn't this mirror life? As a woman in her 60s, I have many stories I could tell, many themes I could mine, many ways to arrange the book of my life. This book, this arrangement, captures my journey through childhood memories, intergenerational trauma, and the depths of love, sometimes told in the first person "I," sometimes in the second person "you," sometimes in the third person "she," as they came to me and through me at the time.

I imagine you could read the haiku straight through to get a sense of that journey, but it will only be a sense–it's the very nature of haiku to be cryptic, to say so much by only saying so little. You could also read each haiku individually, contemplating the images and mining each for its own meaning, apart from the whole. You could rearrange the story by beginning at the end, or dipping into the middle, or flipping through the haiku at random, a sort of "choose your own adventure" story.

However you choose to read these haiku,

my hope, in the end, is for this book not to be about my story alone but yours as well. I've chosen to present only one haiku per page, leaving plenty of white space inside as an invitation to you to engage with the words and images. You can use the book for bibliomancy, opening it randomly and allowing the haiku you find to speak to you of your life at the moment, almost like a deck of divination cards. You can use the haiku as writing prompts or inspiration for your creative expression. You can write your own memoir in haiku.
    This book is for you.
    Make it your own.

PROLOGUE

two ravens' wings touch
lovers' fingers intertwine
holding up the moon

PART I

1

in the silent night
language itself is dreaming
words wake with the dawn

2

listen! the wind swoops
down stealing stories and whisks
them off into night

3

sullen and swollen
with secrets she shakes free from
narrative's shackles

4

in the moonlight she
swims with the archetypes and
dances with the gods

5

the man on the moon
is pulled from the sky into
her muddy embrace

6

she's hitching a ride
on Noah's ark and stealing
stars to light the dark

7

she falls from the sky
found by errant boys who pull
the wings from her back

8

she'll take no baggage
into the unknown as she
leaves her selves behind

9

I lick the thread of
memory and insert it
through the needle of time

10

my mind spits pages
out like an old typewriter
tapped on by a ghost

11

sometimes the past comes
like a speeding chariot
driven by the gods

12

you never forget
the feel of your father's fist
beating in your heart

13

his gaze imposes
a sharp geometry on
her supple body

14

it is the father
who draws blueprints of desire
on his daughter's heart

15

my father and I
bound together by the gut
twin ulcers bleeding

16

the bed of trust is
feathered with betrayal's seeds
ready to blossom

17

she can't be sorry
for sins she did not commit
though her hands still bleed

18

she's walked the past so
often that she's made trenches
in the ground of time

19

my mother's fresh blood
blooms like a bright poppy
on her sun-drenched dress

20

my bubbe's breast caught
on a rusty nail bleeds its
red and wounded milk

21

we will wear the scarves
knitted by our mothers like
cords wrapped 'round our necks

22

we grow into our
ancestors' hardened faces
with each faded dream

23

I am the woman
inside the woman inside
the woman inside

24

mother on a hook
suspended in your psyche
time to cut her down

25

in another part
of her psyche she's dreaming
dreams she can't yet see

26

like water swirling
around an open drain her
story seeks its source

27

in time gardens old
women bitten by memories
flick them off like flies

28

with a pen she pries
open the mouths of the dead
to release their truths

29

a snow globe shatters
her universe in a ball
slipping through God's hands

30

a healer is born
within the uterine walls
of the wound itself

PART II

31

a renegade stream
has split from my life's river
and forged its own course

32

if he'd worn a sign
beware the undertow she
would still have jumped in

33

landlocked on hot sands
the Viking in the desert
longs for icy seas

34

the one-eyed dragon
I love the smell of his breath
and smoke-laced kisses

35

nestled between sheets
of paper their stories lie
in a lovers' tryst

36

her body becomes
a bridge across his abyss
of silent longings

37

lightning splits the tree
two halves float to earth sighing
like spent young lovers

38

to return to you
she will break the string of time
then and then again

39

love multiplies us
it's hard for a woman to
stay true to her selves

40

she can only make
love in the subjunctive mood
as if she were real

41

kept at arm's length her
husband will fox trot away
slow, slow, quick quick, slow

42

my lover's soul leapt
through a hole in heaven and
burrowed inside me

43

she drops her bucket
in the well of his longing and
offers him a drink

44

she loves to watch him
eat a peach and longs to lick
juice from his mustache

he stood on the edge
of his divided self and
dove between the cracks

46

imbibing sadness
staggering in the moonlight
he's drunk on the past

47

he carves the coffin
with the same steady hands used
to shape the cradle

48

myths still roam the plains
as he lassoes his stories
and wrestles them home

49

he stakes his dreams in
the supple soil of her soul
colonizing her

50

he denies her words
are pregnant with a silence
which he has fathered

51

with a hoarder's heart
and miser's lips he turns her
into a beggar

52

she will draw him with
his mouth stitched shut but with blue
eyes leaking stories

53

she ties words like rocks
to his ankles then leads him
to the river's edge

54

she would kill him off
with the stroke of a pen if
she thought he'd stay dead

55

he passed on drinking
from her queen of cups and fell
on his ten of swords

56

a kiss could not bridge
the cosmic distance between
his head and her heart

57

shattered she has learned
too late what's trapped inside you
will always explode

58

you cannot put a
splint on a heart if you are
the one who broke it

59

the way a story
ends changes the meaning of
all that came before

60

he loved her even
more after she walked away
straight into his past

PART III

61

here she comes again
the girl I used to be with
my dreams in her mouth

62

she wears her armor
inside out now to protect
herself from herself

63

she will spend her days
digging up words and bones in
memory's soil

64

she counts her faults like
beads on a rosary worn
smooth by her self-doubts

65

take care not to fall
in someone else's sea and
drown in strange waters

psychic placenta
we all die each night to be
reborn in our dreams

67

night surges like seas
cresting and breaking onto
the shores of morning

68

she prostrates herself
to drink from the trough of truth
and tastes her own tears

69

the biggest lie she
tells herself is that the truth
is overrated

70

she must dismantle
the self she made to love him
wreckage and salvage

71

yes there is even
a need for repair work on
the road not taken

it's never too late
to descend into Hades
to rescue yourself

73

she makes the stars her
loom warping the heavens with
the light of the moon

74

her deft fingers dance
across warp and weft as they
re-spin ancient yarns

75

moonlight catches on
branches and hangs like ripened
fruit ready to fall

the ticking crickets
serenade the harvest moon
counting down to fall

77

red leaves hang on as
autumn takes her final breath
and exhales winter

78

houses sleep soundly
tonight tucked between blankets
of soft downy snow

79

we find our way back
into the light of day by
nursing the darkness

80

writing through thickets
of tangled undergrowth she
comes to a clearing

81

geysers of memory
bursting through the cage of time
a story starts here

82

she tries to live life
backward but the future has
demands of its own

83

it took years to dig
out from the avalanche of
her father's silence

84

she had to swallow
oceans of self-doubt before
learning she could swim

85

love is always here
it is she who's slipped in and
out of its embrace

the wary flower
refolds all dying petals
new bud like a fist

87

she's writing flesh back
on the bones of her story
picked clean by time's lies

88

she unzips her chest
now letting others touch her
bleeding beating heart

89

these thirsty nurslings
cling and whisper at my breast
I will tell their tales

90

love is the only
verb left after language is
annihilated

EPILOGUE

even in endings
a silent voice whispers you
will begin anew

Made in the USA
Las Vegas, NV
08 January 2023

65201944R00066